touch wood

Also by James Dott

A Glossary of Memory (2015, Blind Slough Books)
Another Shore (2019, Kelsay Books)

touch wood

JAMES DOTT
POEMS

WATERSHED PRESS

SEATTLE • 2025

ISBN 979-8-9991654-0-4 (pbk)

FIRST EDITION

PRINTED IN THE United States of America

PHOTOGRAPHS BY Nathan Wirth, sliceofsilence.com
COPYEDITING AND PROOFREADING: Ursula Vaira
DESIGN, TYPOGRAPHY, AND PRODUCTION: Arifin Graham, alarisdesign.com
WATERSHED PRESS LOGO: Roberta Hoffman, robertahoffman.com
PRINTING AND SOFTCOVER BINDERY: Minuteman Press, Spokane, Washington

Watershed Press is an independent bioregional publisher of eco-conscious poetry and prose rooted in the practice of place on both sides of the colonial border in Cascadia.

watershedpress.org

The editorial board of Watershed Press is Adelia MacWilliam, Jason M. Wirth, Dan Clarkson, Ursula Vaira, and Cate Gable.

For more information, in the United States, write to Jason M. Wirth at wirthj@seattleu.edu, and in Canada, write to Adelia MacWilliam at terrapoetics@gmail.com.

Postal inquiries can be sent to Jason M. Wirth, 9807 57th Avenue S., Seattle, WA 98118

In Memory of My Parents
Bob and Nancy Dott

Contents

And this our life
… finds tongues in trees

—William Shakespeare, *As You Like It*

Root, Then Rise

...no one knows or tells from where
the roots of that tree rise

—THE POETIC EDDA ("HÁVAMÁL," VERSE 138)

each name

each name a path
the namer takes
to meet the named

to know ginkgo leaf
alder catkin
spruce cone
how hemlock's bark
will crack with age
each name an ember

coaxed to flame
frayed cedar bark
desiccated twigs of Douglas-fir

a guttered flame
cold clench of smoke
white pine felled
trunk shattered
an acorn succumbed
to rot

each name
a splintered elegy
to pierce
my tongue

Planted Pines at Second Point

Eastern White Pine, *Pinus strobus*
Madison, Wisconsin, Summer Solstice 1971

We went out
wanting to be like Muir
find some grand holiness in Nature
and name it.

We met in the dark
walked the side streets
under maples and elms
skirted the marsh,
passed the iron gate, always open
took the fork up to the grove
overlooking Lake Mendota.
We each chose a pine
planted in the windbreak
when the land was still a farm
and laddered up
to where we could see the bay
still, dark
make the trees lean and swing.

No great storm for us to ride
like Muir did in the Sierras
just blue jays starting their racket below us
crows passing quietly overhead.The sun breaking the soft-hilled horizon
gilding the lakefirst breeze
leans us into easy rhythm
brush of needles
scent of pitch.

Fifty years, still seeking
not the door to wildness flung open
but slipped through quietly

an emptied cone beside the trail
a bright oozing scar high up the trunk
where the bark's been chewed open by porcupine

evergreen, coniferous
needles bundled in fives
maximum height 200 feet at least
not in fifty more years or fifty more
will the white pines we climbed
match those veterans of the storied woods
who lived 450 years
those woods where
you could enter a grove at noon on a summer day
so open beneath the canopy, footsteps quieted by needle duff
where you could spread your arms and never touch two trees
where you could reach around a trunk and your fingers would never meet
the light dim as dusk
those gloried woods
the timber companies
their Paul Bunyans, the homesteaders who came after
felled, cleared, burned.

Tree, Its Roots

Tree, *noun*. 1. General name of the largest of the vegetable kind,
consisting of a firm woody stem springing from woody roots,
spreading above into branches which terminate in leaves.
A *tree* differs from a shrub principally in size. —*Webster's, 1828*
a. A perennial woody plant having a main trunk and usually a distinct crown.
b. A plant or shrub resembling a tree in form or size. —*American Heritage, 2020*
Middle English *tree*. Old English *treo*. Proto-Indo European *deru*: firm, solid, steadfast;
also root of *truth, trust, true*
touch wood let truth solidify

druids, dryads long since exiled from their groves
forests breathe but timber's felled
not beings but commodities
cloned, split, burned green
is a lilac with a single stem thick as an arm a tree?
is the rhododendron with many stems but the arched canopy of an English oak?
is the old ten-inch bonsai pine wired into a wind-bent pose?
or the redwood stump that sent forth a thousand tender shoots all daring to be giants?
is the eighty-thousand-year-old grove of aspen whose trunks all rise
from the same enduring root and die, topple, sprout again, a single tree?

is it in the summing of parts: the anchored root, the steadfast trunk, the air-wrapped branch
each leaf: needle (pointed blunt) or broad palm open to the sun
the seed's suspense
the apical bud's insistent *rise, rise, rise*
the root tip's downward drive
the first dead ring at the heart of the heartwood
the thin sheath of living cells beneath the shielding bark
those sweet offerings from the canopy to the lowest realm
the tributes roots have drawn, lifted to the branches
the leaves, who, in lust with light, perform their mundane, miraculous alchemy of green.

I have dozed in your shade, taken in your out-breath, stolen your fruits
slit your bark to bleed you, snapped your limbs to feed my fire.
I've lived inside your bones
if I could I would learn your tongues
pheromones passed leaf to leaf
sent root to root
touch wood
trust encircle us

A Confusion of Pines

You will begin to think I manufacture pines at my pleasure.

—DAVID DOUGLAS TO HIS MENTOR, WILLIAM JACKSON HOOKER

Naming the Tree

Douglas-fir—*Pseudotsuga menziesii*

Remarkably tall, unusually straight...thickly clad to the very ground, wide-spreading pendent branches...Nature's most graceful object.

—DAVID DOUGLAS

635
First fire
seedlings, you will wither in the shade
need flame to open the canopy.
Elders must burn and fall.
Next mist, rain, thin soil, and sun.
Some of you will be eaten, others will wither
a few will reach toward sun.

Since that burn
some of you assembled 1400 rings,
a few were felled by wind and slides
swept into rivers, washed to sea
where you drifted for years.

Throughout your range
the original Indigenous names
that drew the namer toward the heart of you
those names, those who spoke those names
long since sunk in needle duff.
Your buds
perfectly formed rusty embers
flare into yellow-green needles
each spring.

1791
Archibald Menzies,
ship's surgeon and naturalist on the *Discovery*,
duties: bleeding, amputation, collecting seeds.
He first found you on Vancouver Island
thought you a pine,
menziesii for him.

Thirty years later David Douglas,
a gardener's apprentice at Scone Palace in Scotland,
was recruited to collect and catalog
new plants in America.
Billy, a Scottish terrier, his constant companion.
He gathered your seeds in the Oregon country,
sowed your gospel like Chapman with the apple.
Only at home in his joy: encountering new plants.

Spread now, far beyond your original range,
an ornamental, an invasive, a cash crop.

Your needles persist for eight years,
leave scars on the twig when they drop.

1794/1834

Menzies was among the first whites
to summit Mauna Loa on Hawaii.
When Douglas came forty years later
Hawaiians still remembered Menzies,
"the red-faced man who cut off men's arms and legs
and gathered grass."
Douglas too made the summit
but went snow-blind, wandered lost for days.
He also climbed Mauna Kea, Hawaii's other taller peak.
While climbing it, Douglas remarked in his journal:
the grassy flanks of the mountain abound with wild cattle,
offspring of stock left here by Capt. Vancouver,
and which now prove a very great benefit to this island.
Neither Menzies nor Douglas could untangle your taxonomy,
knotted with misnamings:
Oregon pine, Douglas spruce, *taxifolia,* "yew-leaf"
but not pine, not spruce, not a yew.
Your own genus with cousins in Asia,
that stockier sibling in the Rockies: *glauca,* gray
like Billy's muzzle after years of collecting.
Mature needles appear dark green to nearly black
depending on the light, the distance from the eye.

2000 BCE/2000 CE
Your logs, smoothed and bleached by your drifting years,
washed up on beaches in Hawaii,
were split and burned, chopped and carved
into long, double-hulled, dugout canoes.

Few old growth groves remain,
few new stands will reach their age.
Clear-cut replaced wildfire to open forests for your young.
Investors demand returns on shorter terms than centuries.

What shall we call you where two or three or more of you
    are gathered?
A copse, a stand, a grove, unit in a tree farm, a community of
    chlorophyll and lignin?
A congregation—rooted, reaching toward light, ready to burn?

Your thick bark resists fire
heartwood rose, sapwood white when first cut, ambers with age.
You've been milled into beams, studs peeled for plywood, cut young
    for Christmas trees.
Your needles are flattened, blunt, soft in the hand.

1834/1934

Walking the flanks of Mauna Loa Douglas fell into a bull pit
was trampled and killed by a captured bull,
offspring of cattle left by *Discovery.*
He'd been warned of the traps,
walked past them, turned back.
Some believed a bull hunter named Gurney
struck him with an ax, stole his purse, shoved him in.
Searchers found Billy thirty yards past the pits,
fiercely guarding his master's bundle,
clothes, notebook,
no money.
That place in the grassy scrub is called
Ka lua kauka, "Doctor's Pit."
One hundred years after his death
local Scots erected a memorial marker,
planted two hundred of you.
Your needles have a sweet, resinous scent
when crushed.

Radicle

the part of a seed
that will become
the main root

so *root* begins
drills down
cleaves stone
drinks darkness
raises the dead
branching tendrils
fungi's mycelial nets
the warp and weft of *forest*
learns soil's tongue

one
from many
many into
one

King of Pines

Sugar Pine, *Pinus lambertiana* (in Umpqua: *nát-cleh*)

In the tobacco pouches of the Indians I found the seeds of a remarkably large pine which they eat as nuts, learned it existed in the mountains to the south.

—DAVID DOUGLAS

David,
from that moment
enamored with tales of its great height, its enormous cones
you sought this *king*
largest of pines   easily reaching 160 feet
female cones biggest of any conifer: 12 to 24 inches long

(October 25, 1827   Umpqua River, Oregon Country)
Reached my long-wished Pinus
new or strange things   seldom fail to make great impressions
lest I should never see my friends to tell them   of this most beautiful
    immense tree
dimensions of one blown down: 18 feet through, length 215 feet,
Remarkably straight   bark uncommonly smooth   yields a great
    quantity of bright amber gum branches pendulous, cones hanging from
    their points like small sugarloaves in a grocer's shop

Putting myself in possession of three cones   (all I could)
nearly brought my life to an end unable to climb or hew down any
took my gun, clipping them from branches with ball
8 Indians came at the report of my gun painted with red earth
armed with bows, arrows, spears of bone, flint knives
seemed anything but friendly
endeavored to explain what I wanted
seemed satisfied sat down to smoke
no sooner done   I perceived one string his bow
another sharpen his knife
Cocked my gun   pulled one of my pistols   was determined to fight

stood ten minutes looking at them   they at me   without a word
till one   who seemed the leader   made sign for tobacco
which I said they should get on condition   of fetching me some cones
they went   as soon as out of sight   picked up my three cones
made quick retreat
gained camp at dusk

David,
Can only guess what tales those eight Umpqua told of that day
the strange white man who shot down *nát-cleh cones*
how your aim was excellent   how they admired your guns
how they were glad to see your backside   relieved no one had to
    die that day

You named it *lambertiana* for Aylmer Bourke Lambert
British taxonomist who compiled *A Description of the Genus Pinus*
now outdated since he (like you) lumped spruce and deodar cedar in
    with the pines
incomplete without this tree
and the western white, the white-bark, the limber, the Ponderosa,
    the shore
Why not use the Umpqua name—you noted it in your journal—
…in that place, that time…nát-cleh was its name

David,
The tallest living sugar pine (255 feet)
grows in Douglas County, Oregon (not named for you)
survived girdling by vandals with chainsaws back in 2000
Nearly four hundred years since it sprouted
from a seed loosed from a cone on its mother-tree
when the Pilgrims were felling its cousins, eastern white pine
to ship back to England to pay the debt for their journey

Such cones!
the ones my mother gifted me to share with my students
after retiring found in a box in the basement,
thinking *I don't need these anymore*
used them as kindling watching them smolder,
flare through the glass door of the wood stove
only then remembered   she told me she'd collected them
in a campground on the North Umpqua
the May before I was born

David,
next fall
I'll camp along the Umpqua
search for a sugar pine who's just shed her cones
collect three
to keep

Roots

Theirs is not
the lighted world
they go below
probe soil's night
branch
work around stones
fret at bedrock cracks
branch
drink and twine together
store the sap
branch
spread deeper farther
from the center
the seed squirrels missed
always gravity's allure

thick as torsos then thighs
forearms fingers
narrowing to net strands
fine as spiders' silk
where root tip ends
and soil begins
only an atom's breadth

step carefully
when they breach
entwine the trail
re-submerge
their world entering ours
only when wind-thrown
undercut by road work
flooded up whole
when the river crests

they are the anchor
they are the well
the way down
that leads back
to the leaf-lit
canopy

The Water is Wide

Pinus contorta

Wood soft, spongy, with abundance of rosin. Little can be said
in favour of this tree either for ornament or as a useful wood.

—DAVID DOUGLAS

The water is wide, I cannot cross over

Clatsop Spit, last land before open ocean
wave-break roar over foredune
dog nosing ahead
as the sandy trail twists through shore pines,
low, bent, lichened boughs.
David Douglas collected here, 1825,
trekking in by game or native trail
with Billy, before his muzzle had gone gray,
barking on at a squirrel scolding him,
"Pillillooeet, Pillillooeet"
small, dark back, rufous belly, tufted ears
            Douglas squirrel

Neither have I wings to fly

        Contorta for "very twisted"
        from its winding root come
        turn and *torment, torch* and *torture.*
        Needles bundled into pairs
        twins or lovers, twos and twos
        whorled 'round each branch

Give me a boat that can carry two

Samples collected
"on swampy ground near the seacoast"
shipped to John Loudon at the Herbarium in London
who published the first description in his
The Trees and Shrubs of Britain
Douglas called it:
>   *twisted branched pine*

>   *And both shall row, my love and I*

Loudon noted its abundance
from Cape Disappointment to the north
south to Cape Lookout
as if he knew the country
when all he had were maps
and the labeled, dried specimens Douglas sent
and David's tales over whisky, ale
when he was back in London,
already yearning to be gone.
No seeds yet planted so Loudon could include
notes on the living tree.

>   *A ship there is and she sails the sea*

"His return was expected by the very ship
that brought the tidings of his horrible death…
falling into a pit made for catching wild bulls
on the Sandwich Islands,"
tormented, trampled
by the bull already trapped there
gored by its twisted horn.
Loudon didn't tell
how Billy would have barked and barked and barked.

She's loaded deep as deep can be

One species   two variants

Shore pine   Lodgepole pine

I know not if I sink or swim

On his final voyage stuck in Monterey, California
impatient in the summer heat
all the flowers done, nothing more to collect
waiting for a ship bound for Vancouver or Sitka
but, "the wine was very excellent"
the ladies, "very amiable … good teeth … fine dark eyes"
he settled for a berth on a ship bound for Hawaii.

I leaned my back against an oak

Shore pine is the contorted one
leaning leeward
pruned by the salty winds
of winter storms
on rocky headlands and old dunes

Thinking it a trusted tree

I have not found the tree's Indigenous name
trails that twist and turn
through shore pine shade
fade out in beach grass
too damp to twist into a torch's wick
and light a way

But first it bent and then it broke

In Chinook Jargon, the tongue of trade
it's *Lagum Stik*, Pitch Stick
stik being wood or
wooden or tree or forest
you find little precision in pidgin
stik skin is bark,

its wood pops, sparks, as it burns
pitch pine

So did my love prove false to me

Then there's lodgepole pine
tall, straight, and slender
no contortions here
successful in drier, higher soils
on the lee side of the Cascades
ranging through the Rockies
into the Black Hills
cut and stripped of branches, bark
for tipi poles or fence posts

Oh wail, wail along the shore

Rumors say Douglas had a son, named David Finlay, shot, stripped,
    and scalped
by a band of Blackfeet when he was twenty-two
his mother Josette, sixteen, when Douglas
made visits to old Spokane House up the Colville valley, 1826,
(nothing in his journals about her) gently rolling hills
copses of lodgepole pine
    David, did you *know* her? Or is this just apocryphal?
    But if you did was it love or lust
    or rape?

And wail, wail up on the hill

Often in even-aged stands growing close packed
as the hair on a Scottish terrier
until thinned or cleared by chainsaws, fires
like those infernal tempests
that incinerated Yellowstone in '88
miles of fallen forest, charred ghosts of a greener once
its cones stay closed for years on the branch
until opened by the heat of conflagration
    Pinus incenda

No comfort now can e'er be found

Some botanists say *contorta* refers to the paired needles
how each twists away from, turns back toward the other
like conjoined twins
forever seeking the impossible
how one can never be the other,
yet never be
parted

Since my love and I came unbound

How one can always be taken as the other
        map and territory
        sex and love
        the collector, his collection
        the torch and its tortured flame
        how the name binds
        namer to the named

The Dead are Many

Six Ways to Kill a Tree

Cut Surface Treatment
Make cuts around the trunk with an ax or hatchet.
Swab herbicide on cuts.

Injection Treatment
Make small cuts every 2 to 6 inches around the trunk.
Inject herbicide into cuts.

Stump Treatment
After cutting a tree down pour herbicide on the fresh stump
to prevent sprouting.

Basal Bark Treatment
Apply herbicide to the lower 12 inches of the tree's bark
from early spring to mid-fall.

Foliage Treatment
Spray herbicide on leaves of trees.

Soil Treatment
Spray or scatter herbicide on the soil around roots of targeted tree.

—COMPILED FROM STATE UNIVERSITIES' EXTENSION BULLETINS

Bark

Not the bark of our embarkation
not the barque you'd board to begin the voyage
half-sunk in obscurity
its rigging scheme, its history
kept afloat by aficionados of the age of sail
not that barque
but tree hide flensed from logs
of straight-growing conifers
felled to make its masts
had good speed, rose well to the wind

used as a whaler, grain hauler
and sometimes a slaver.

And not the bark with yelp and snarl
that makes the speech of dogs, their kin,
the woodland wolves, but the pelts of the trees
where they whelped and roamed and howled
before it was all peeled away.

Bark, the skin of trees
armor against disease, injury, desiccation
if cut it bleeds, heals over in scabby lumps
can be damaged by the elements
sun-scald, frost-crack.
Some barks stand up to fire, others char through.

The green and gold of sapling bark does not last
it darkens or fades to new hues
birch-white to black oak-black
grades of gray, variations on brown
with overlays of lichen, furs of moss.

Smooth at first
but for the nicks and slits of lenticels
airways so the inner bark can breathe
there the cambium builds the tree
a wall where meristem cells decide and divide.
On the inner surface: woody xylem shafts
that lift water to the leaves.
On the outer: phloem cells
to carry sweet sap to the trunk, the roots.

The bark a sheath from root tip to twig end
to cover the delicate cambium.
Bark swells, stretches, as the tree gains
girth so splits, peels, flakes off
creates terrains both possible and surreal:
deep arroyos dissecting mesas,
braided streams through glacial outwash cross-furrowed labyrinths
from which there is no exit
sinews of current that divide
embrace boulders, then re-twine downstream,
parallel ridges of black basalt
half covered by wind-blown snow
plates that curl and finally fall away
dark icebergs swept off by storm.

Some chew through it to the sapwood
even eat the bark itself, though difficult to digest
some hide within it, others hunt them there
porcupine and spider, nuthatch, mite.
For us: canoe hulls, roof tiles, fibers for baskets
soaked and pounded it makes a cloth
source of cork, aspirin, cinnamon
we blaze it to mark our way
carve in our first love's name
burn it when the wood is gone

chew it off with de-barker blades
chop it into bark rock, bark chips
grind it finer, make a mulch.

When the soul of the cambium has disembarked
the bark is released
and though it may cling for years
in time it tatters, tears open, sloughs off
in sheets, strips, chunks joins the ground, where
beetles, wood lice, worms
work it down
work it down
to duff.

Their Shade is Deep

Western Hemlock, *Tsuga heterophylla*

Abundant on the woody parts of the North-West coast larger than any
found on the Atlantic side of the Continent; absent in the interior.

—DAVID DOUGLAS

Below the sun-blown canopy the shade is deep
      the dead are many
Queek-queek-queek
a nesting woodpecker cries alarm.
Two boys enter swinging sticks, leap over crumbling logs
do-see-do between
standing hemlock poles, thick as their arms, legs
      young trees that did not finish the race to light
branches, tops long rotted off, wood beneath the tattered bark
      all sponge.
The boys thrust and parry, drop their weapons
      each grab a trunk to shake, shove and lever loose
         watch it softly fall.

Short uneven needles, bright yellow-green at budding
darkening with age, *heterophylla*.
Lead tips droop, recall
ascent from soil and nurse logsbow to fallen elders, the younger
   deadlook in wonder at how far their trunks have reached.
Small cones, shallow grooves in a thin bark
      color of a barn swallow's breast banking at the forest edge
first blush of rust on the ax head the boys left out.

With age lichen spreads a gray wash up trunks
      sprouts even in heavy shade.
How did this homely tree of northwest woods
get knotted with that stream-side herb, *Conium maculatum*
      the "hemlock" of Socrates' demise
      from whose juice his fatal drink was brewed?

Conium, konos, cone, top, whirling, vertigo
        the dizziness the poison brings
maculatum, "spotted"
        green stems splotched with purple stains.
Its feathered leaves echo delicate branches
        each leaflet a tree in profile
        or a cone halved on its axis.

After Socrates drank they walked him round
until the potion numbed his feet, his legs,
began to spin his head, then sat him down to wait
        Plato, Crito, Simmias, loyal students at his side
        in those final hours he continued teaching
        declared the living arise from the dead
        proved to them the unseen part of each lives on
        after the body, unchanging, unchanged
        vowed to meet them in Elysium.
Or maybe he just told them that
        to hedge their grief
knowing he was really
whirling down into the deep shadow and shade
at the root of everything.

No poison in the tree
though a black dye can be made
        if you steep the bark in urine.
The young shoot tips
can be eaten in emergency
the pitch chewed like gum
        or spread on the chest to ease a cold.
Useful for interior trim, furniture, framing
        excellent for paper pulp
as firewood—hard to split.

Its eastern sisters have their own executioner
        the tiny wooly adelgid, an aphid native to East Asia

pierces twigs with its mouth parts and sucks the sap.
With no predators, no resistance
    Tsuga caroliniana and *canadensis*
may go the way of chestnut and elm
their needles go gray, die, and drop, trunks follow
    the canopy will open, black birch come in.

The boys grab up their sticks,
exit yelling
    Queek, queek, queek.
Sunlight, slants   between trunks   touches the forest floor,
    first time since September,
where logs of those long down
    nurse
    a fresh draught of hemlock.

Acorn

White Oak, *Quercus alba*

The acorn is large, handsome, ovate, almost an inch long;
one of the largest, most abundant, and useful species

—DAVID DOUGLAS

Listen
how your footsteps soften
where the path passes over the white oak's fallen trunk
surrendering to earth so small a sound
lost behind the blur of rain
an acorn gone from green to brown
loosed downward strikes, rebounds grounds out among leaves shed
on dampened loam
a child's hand closing
warm
around a treasured stone

the hard seed wall splits so small
a sound
embryo unfists
fingers lifting to let you peer
at the precious thing cupped within

there is no Eden only soil's black heaven
some small protection from fruits of others' sins
parching drought drowning flood
sinking taint of herbicides
the muted miracle still may come
root-tip piercing darkness
twin cotyledons—first leaves—pressing upward
to part the earth the air
Listen, all that
fell before
will be undone

After the Equinox

Big Leaf Maple, *Acer macrophyllum*

Its large foliage and elegant racemes of yellow fragrant flowers contrast
delightfully with the pines by which it is surrounded.

—DAVID DOUGLAS

after the equinox
the big leaf maple wakes
from winter's skeletal slumber,
when thrashed in gales
neighbors fell,
branches ripped away,
and rot began deep in its heartwood,

sufficient light, warmth arrive
sap is lifted
pregnant buds spill flowers,
yellow-green pagodas
dangling earthward
their tiered lanterns briefly lit,
their incense enticing flies, beetles, bees,
"come fertilize, it is time
for sex and resurrection,"

robins chase in crazed courtship,
crash into leafing brambles,
flickers tap territories,
crows strip moss and lichens
from the maple's limbs,
so soft for lining nests,
last year's spin of seeds
push aside stones and arise from the soil

leaf buds split
slowly unclench fists,
relaxing fingers open
perfect palms of joyful green
un-torn, unscarred, unaware of the incipient rot,
unfold to summer's lush incarnation
growing darkness, the fall,
another life

Speak Their Names

Again the dream
the path bends, arcs back, a branch in the wind
takes me in and in
through young sun-dappled stands
to deep-shaded old growth
acer, alnus, tsuga
gentle brush of branch tips, leaves
taxus, willow, pine
vast lung of earth
the cycle of each breath takes years.

So tired now, still
I trudge deeper in
follow her story of the kettled dell
where *Yggdrasil,* the great ash
still towers.

Night falls, moonless/stars all blocked by leaves and limbs
at last the path leads gently down
to that vale where she said it grows
but no trunk rises from the fog settled in the hollow.
I glimpse a stump so wide ten could lie across it head to foot to head
so freshly cut the bleeding sap pools over the rings
too closely grown to ever count
all around it splintered branches, the bucked and shattered trunk

And there it nightly ends
the bed a clear-cut plain
windows open on blank unmoving air
asking why am I called again, again in witness?

Tonight I do not wake

have fallen exhausted, tangled in its bones
cheek and ear crushed to bark
from below the tumbled dark
a whisper rises: *picea, cedar, yew*
a murmur: *sequoia, apple, oak*
sudden burst of shoots from soil
shove past, rush skyward
lapse of time awry
soon saplings, suddenly trees
who reach and reach
above the fog.

Slightly swaying branches
shadow me in green
I breathe the exhaled air
speak their names
acer, alnus, tsuga,
hemlock, ginkgo, ash.

Force of Fiery Green

An ash I know there stands,
Yggdrasil is its name,
a tall tree, showered
with shining drops.
From there come the dews
that fall in the valleys.
It stands forever green
over the Fates' dark wells.

—THE POETIC EDDA, ("VÖLUSPÁ," VERSE 19)

For Hildegard von Bingen *viriditas*
was a "force of fiery greenness" that flowed
like sap through all the living.

Ginkgo

Ginkgo biloba—Takayama, Japan, 1991

A light rain falls, low clouds hide the mountains,
wisps of mist cling to the ridges the city has grown onto.
The van swings off the street and heads uphill to Takayama
    Agricultural High School.
A row of young ginkgoes, just beginning to turn,
lines the curving drive.
A few leaves litter the ground—
Yellow-green striated lobes, a simple symmetry, *biloba,*
Darwin's *living fossils,* one of the first among trees.
Maiden-hair tree, once found world-wide,
thought extinct until found in remote temple grounds in China.
From the Japanese *ginkyo,* silver apricot,
an ancient medicinal, its fruit and leaves ~~used to~~
used to improve circulation, brain function,
fight yeast infections, relieve asthma.

On my lap a small wrapped box holds a gift for my mother,
a ginkgo-leaf-with-fruit pin, carved from the wood.
There's a ginkgo in my parents' yard
that after twenty years finally flowered, turned out to be female
bearing fruits that smelled like vomit when they dropped.
Two nights ago in Kanazawa I ate its nutty seed
a pale green orb hidden in yellow egg custard.
After the meal we'd lingered at the low table
sipping sake, recalling the day,
our visit in a first-grade classroom
two students presented us with a garland of a thousand cranes,
said in unison, "We have studied the bombing of Hiroshima
and give you this, in peace."

David, our tour leader, spoke, "I've been to Pearl Harbor,
Soldier's Field, Los Alamos and White Sands,
Hiroshima and Nagasaki...but today, those kids...."
He didn't say more,
staring into the shadows beneath the table.
Into that silence the story of Sadako came back to me,
the Hiroshima school girl who loved to run,
but could not out-pace the leukemia
that burned in her bones,
all the cranes she folded.

The van slows near the top of the drive,
My grandfather knew the ginkgo first from fossil leaves
and then from leaves shed by a pair of ginkgoes
on the grounds of a Tulsa oilman's mansion.
Years later he saved them from the bulldozer's blade—
had them moved to his office grounds.
He is gone, ashes under black Oklahoma sod, but they still stand,
scattering bright yellow every autumn.
The van stops. We get out. I look over the tops of the ginkgoes,
across the valley, the mist has drifted away
so we can see a gold-roofed temple shining, even in the gray.
We ask its name.
Our driver tells us,
"Sukyo Mahikari Shrine.
People go there and are healed of their disease."

Yew

Taxus

The natives on the Columbia prefer this wood to any other
for making their bows; branches pendulous; a handsome tree;
plentiful in dark low valleys.

—DAVID DOUGLAS

The poisoned bow of shadow and shade, a conifer with no female
cone, a berry-like *aril* instead, a tiny blood-red bowl, holds a poison
seed birds can pass unscathed. Slow growing, resprouts from trunk,
root, branch, inhabits the understory's shadow and shade.

Wide-spread but not common in the wild, find yew in cemeteries,
churchyards, planted and pruned in gardens, plantations of clones in
China raised for their potent taxanes, beneath old-growth hemlocks
and red-cedars, in crosswords, three letters, denizen of shadow
and shade.

The old goddesses, *Hekate, Artemis, Banbha, Diana,* their more
ancient elders, embedded in yew branch and yew root and hollowed
bole, rotted out, fallen, regrown, their amulets and invocations,
appearances in dream, so much smoke whispered through shadow
and shade.

Long bows shaved from yew, heartwood facing paler sapwood,
could send an arrow through armor, kept the English out of Wales,
victory at Agincourt, archers grew twisted spines, longer left arms,
grooves in fingers, groves gone for bow staves, empty of shadow
and shade.

Taxol, from taxanes in Pacific yew bark, a poison arrow aimed at
solid tumors in lungs, breasts, ovaries, for this new weapon bark
hunters hiked miles through old-growth searching out yews, they
girdled trunks, stripped off their harvest, so many fallen in shadow
and shade.

Yews planted by Irish saints bled if cut, the culprit, cursed, dropped dead from poison. At six archers began their training, small bows first then larger, larger, building strength. Their arrows flew until they drew no more, bow outlasting bowman, aimed into shadow and shade.

Not every arrow meets its mark, many fall, do not resprout. The way upward and the way downward are one. If the bow still flexes, draw back, eat the aril not the seed. In spring seeds birds have passed will germinate, breaths of golden pollen rise from shadow and shade.

Red Alder

Alnus rubra

After a gentle rain
the alder fell across the road;
the neighbors with their chainsaws
bucked up the trunk,
cleared one lane.

It grew on the uphill side,
leaned into the gap
above the roadway
not the largest along this stretch,
not the smallest,
its bark no longer the glossy gray-green
it was as a sapling and the road was new,
muddy malachite or wetted serpentine,
nicked by lenticels of the color it would become:
a smooth ashen gray daubed by white lichen,
felted by yellow moss.

Not a weed, but weed-like,
a native pioneer, prefers the riverbank,
but being a prolific seeder,
takes the open ground after a burn
or blowdown, a flood, a slide,
a clear-cut, or a road.
Grows fast with enough light and rain, yet
we do not marvel
at an alder's age, or girth, or height.

For a time it gives its lead to *wood* and *flat*,
creek, *brook* and *grove*,
as it prepares the way for its own demise,
making shade, enriching earth.

Root nodules home to bacteria,
that breathe nitrogen into soil,
ensuring the success of sprouting cedar, spruce, and Douglas-fir.

Von Bongard, in his St. Petersburg herbarium,
named it *Alnus rubra,*
from specimens collected in Sitka,
when Alaska was still on Russia's books.

Nuttal called it *oregona,*
encountered as he birded and botanized
through the Oregon country, 1834–35.
Rubra grew in favor,
color of winter twigs, dye from the inner bark.

Doubly red, alder roots
back to *aller, alor,* to *el-*
a reddish-brown hue
as in elm and elk.
The alder's white living wood
when cut
bleeds to rusty red.

It had it's time,
a middling, human length.
When winds tried to break it,
it only bent; when rain and rain sought to drown it,
its roots reached deep and drank.

After the county road crew
cleared away the rest of it,
a sapling hemlock
pinned beneath the alder's trunk
sprang back
unbroken.

Cones

Douglas collected thousands, shot them down when too high for climbing,
pried them apart, precisely described each one:
sessile, ovate, pointed
pendulous, cylindrical, blunt

containers for the stuff of sex
the tiny males
packed with pollen
released to the mercy
of gravity and wind
so much is made
that always some will drift
to female cones, tube in
to the ovules
penetrate the egg
and these cones will swell
with their growing wealth of seeds

tight green
going golden
homely brown
dangling
standing
fused to branch

in time
even the miser's fist
unclenches

torn loose by the gale
disassembled by beak and tooth
by paw and hand
the tithe taken
the rest
let fall

Fallen, Felled

Gilgamesh and Enkidu stood there marveling at the forest
gazing at the lofty cedars ...
They saw the Mountain of Cedar ...
the cedar proffered its abundance
its shade was sweet and full of delight ...
... Gilgamesh slew Humbaba, the forest's guardian ...
the mountains did quake
the hillsides did tremble ...
Gilgamesh went down to trample the forest.
He discovered the secret abode of the gods,
Gilgamesh felling the trees, Enkidu choosing the timber.

—GILGAMESH

The Never Named

What use
for that place in memory each name holds
the key that opens
locks out
our knowing

Romeo   Juliet
Montague   Capulet
Tree Farm   Clear-cut

What need for the path to follow back
to the canyoned pattern of the bark
the cone nestled in needle duff
the apple's blushing swell
the last unblighted grove
roots entangled in the world below

What of all whose names
have been expunged
gone to drought and fire
herbicides, adelgids,
saw chains, goats' teeth

What of the never-named
who lie
in unmarked graves:
No One
Nothing

Cedars: True or False

The Greeks used *kedrus,* the Romans *cedrus*
to name both the true cedars
and the junipers of the Mediterranean.
Later any evergreen with aromatic wood
was *cedar.*
The name fallen from precision into confusion
clumps trees more different than like, more distant than close kin,
true cedars have needles,
false cedars: cypress, juniper have flattened sprays instead.

The true cedar of Lebanon,
native to the mountains of the Middle East,
where the holy grove of Enlil reached to heaven
that Gilgamesh and Enkidu sought and found
not for pilgrimage but plunder, slaughtered its guardian,
hacked and felled the tallest trees
and rafted them downriver to build the great gate at Uruk.

In retribution for their desecration
Enkidu grew ill and died within days,
and the great Gilgamesh, felled by grief,
wept and wandered in the loss of his other self.

And so began the cutting, for cities and fleets of ships,
that sailed for trade and into war, for temples, stables, inns.

In the Levant Victoria had a wall built
around the grove called, *Cedars of God*
to keep out sapling-eating goats,
but then came World War I and the British Army,
needing railroad ties, cut into that grove again.

No cedars on the slopes now

no roots, no shade,
mountains shed soil in heavy rains,
summers heating up.

Dry ridges
where only goats
browse weeds.

Fire on the Ridge

Juniper, *Juniperus monosperma*—Gila National Forest, New Mexico, 1978

At the edge
where cliff plunges into blackness,
the thick bleached bones of a fallen juniper burn in the night.

After hours of speed-hiking from the closest road,
the two of us each hauling a shovel, a Pulaski, a five-gallon
    bladder bag,
threading around boulders of crumbling granite, between pinyon
    and juniper,
scrambling up the last gully, headlamps dimming, we arrive.
Our orders: Contain. Control. Monitor until out.
Don says, "Hell, this ain't going anywhere."
We dump our loads, drink water, and wait.
Empty our bladder bags, our own bladders, and wait.

The trunk flames open,
the sun, captured by needles, hoarded in wood,
escapes into the cool dark.
Ring by ring it burns:
the thin rings of dry years, the wider rings of wetter years,
the rings of the years Apache hunters tracked elk and deer,
the ring of the year Coronado came seeking Cibola and its gold—
the stories he followed north led him through lands
where there was a heavier glow than gold in the Earth,
an ancient fire in the stone, Uranium—
the rings of the years those who tapped that power and
gambled it away to the one who always wins—Entropy,
the rings of the years mines slashed into these mountains,
the ring of the year they made Geronimo pose in a Cadillac,
the rings of the years the lower hills were cut clear for firewood,
the rings of the years of the floods and slides that followed,

the rings of the years the trees grew back,
and the black scar from the fire that swept the ridge in '58,
and the deep rose-red of the heart wood,
all the rings linked in incense of juniper.

Near dawn the crackling ceases,
the coals float a last flicker then drown,
a waning moon, the spilled swath of stars,
crickets, and a low wind spreading smoke.

Elegy for Western Redcedar

Thuja plicata

The seine is resorted to as a means of taking salmon in the still parts of the stream with great success; spindle-formed pieces of the wood of *Thuya plicata*, which is very buoyant, attached to the net by the smaller end, act as corks. The rope of the net is made from the bark of a species of *Salix*, some of *Thuya*.

—DAVID DOUGLAS

I

In steep draws under second-growth spruce and hemlock,
old stumps of western red cedar crumble,
sprout licorice fern and huckleberry;
light leaks through the distant canopy
closing around the ghosts of their trunks.
Notches cut for steps and springboards
where loggers climbed and stood
still show on the stumps.
Since the old ones fell few seeds sprouted, fewer grew.

II

Thuja, Greek for a distant cousin, long ago renamed *plicata,*
plaited, not needles but flattened sprays of emerald braids.
Not a 'true cedar' but a cypress, *arbor vitae,* "tree of life,"
its small female cones, first soft green then woody brown,
⠀⠀⠀release paper-winged seeds
whose unremembered flights and scattered landings
began the grove.

III

Those first in this land say if you lean against it you gain its strength,
call it "long life maker."
Say long ago there was a man
who did so much for his people that when he died
a benevolent spirit grew this tree from his grave to honor his gifts:
its bark easily stripped and twisted, woven,

or braided for ropes, nets, hats, robes,
its wood so carvable and clean splitting:
bowls, canoes, paddles, house planks, memorial poles,
the bent-wood box from which Raven freed the moon,
masks of the Wild Woman of the Woods, lips pursed for her call:
    uu hu uu—
she'd grab children who wandered too far and toss them into the
    basket on her back.
Those first here gave a kind of grace, for forgiveness and permission
    before taking.

IV

The top cut, the undercut, and back cut complete;
the foreman's call as the trunk begins to lean, the crew leaps down,
    away
the final creak and snap, gravity grips, it leans and goes
shearing neighbors' branches, crushes through the undergrowth,
    thunders the unrelenting ground.
Brief shower of needles, fallers' joyous howls echoing off the silence,
    back slaps, the crew scrambling up to assemble on the cut,
saw dust, wood chips clinging to grinning faces, sweat-damp arms,
no prayer, no thanks, just a job-of-work:
a tree, a log, board feet of lumber,
a few dollars in their pockets on Saturday night
for beer, a bath, the brothel, beer, the brawl, more beer
back to camp on Sunday, hungover, bruised, broke.

V

Now the axe heads and
two-man cross-cut saw blades are rusted, all sold for scrap,
but for one that hangs above the fireplace
at the Logger's Inn up on the highway,
its blade painted in bright acrylics:
a log shack, rhododendrons blooming beside a creek,
uncut woods beyond.

The shingles and shakes, window frames, posts and boats
the trunk became
have rotted by now, what remains:
lining of a cedar chest, soundboard of a guitar,
resinous scent of heartwood, a note's woody timbre,
Thuja plicata,
western redcedar,
Arbor manes
Tree-of-ghosts

Log Yard

Douglas on his fir:
The wood may be found very useful for a variety of domestic purposes:
the young slender ones exceedingly well adapted for making ladders
and scaffold poles; the larger timber for more im- portant purposes;
while at the same time the rosin may be found deserving attention.

limbless corpses stripped to pale cambium, graded, sorted,
stacked in house-high, block-long decks, await their afterlife

log ships in the anchorage, basalt-black river pocked by rain
two berthed for loading at the pier, holds empty, cranes ready

downriver, upriver mill stacks spew rendered steam and
pulp stench that rises, pools along the underbelly of cloud

the shale-grey sky empties itself, vomiting a tainted meal,
the blur of downpour floods the ruts eroded by log trucks

that splash minute by minute into the yard where a swarm
of claw-mouthed stackers open wide, bite each load off, then

back and turn, speed on, carry them to growing decks according to
log length, diameter, efficiently stacking to the prescribed height

scattered shreds of skin are tidied into piles on the asphalt,
shoveled up for later use as bio-mass fuel or soil supplements

what were trees only wood now, ready to be stowed, freighted, broken
on unloading in a Chinese port (loss by breakage calculated into price)

or, if surviving whole, to be bucked and ripped, rough cut for use
in constructing forms for concrete buildings, used once or twice then

scrapped for fuel or cobbled into a workers' shanty town or, instead,
milled into door or cabinet frames installed in high-rise condominiums,

or peeled for plywood, each ring flattened, glued to the next year
then hidden under a veneer of a more aesthetic, tight-grained wood

on the gravel verge at the log yard's entrance fallen trunk shards,
lost bits of bark, swept aside by passing tires, blacken in the rain

Where Spruce Comes In

Pinus menziesii (Picea sitchensis, *Sitka Spruce) possesses one great advantage over*

P. douglasii *(Douglas-Fir) by growing to a very large size in poor, thin, damp soils; and even in rocky places, where there is scarcely a sufficiency of earth to cover the horizontal wide-spread- ing roots, their growth is so far from being retarded that they exceed one hundred feet high and eight feet in circumference ... it would thrive in such places in Britain. It would become a useful and large tree. The wood is remarkably fine, white, smooth, and regularly grained.*

I regret that all the seeds of this truly magnificent tree were lost and could not be replaced.

—DAVID DOUGLAS

West Through the Coast Range

Sitka Spruce—*Picea sitchensis*

Mile Post 45 to 14
Driving west out of the city, late summer heat,
Sunset Highway climbs into coast range clear-cuts
holding last purple blooms of foxglove and fireweed,
vine maple starting to smolder into orange and red,
darker green of older stands, mostly Doug-fir, some hemlock.

Through the tunnel at the first summit
named for the ODOT worker
who was killed when the roof collapsed
after weeks of heavy rain
where that kid held his breath a few years back,
passed out, and crashed head-on into another car.
It only takes ten seconds to get through it
—so how did that happen?
Miraculously no deaths.

My daughter surfaces from her phone, glares at the forest,
"I hate trees…there are just, like, so many of them,"
this from the girl who can tell a pine from a fir from a hemlock.
I say, "I love trees," and let my litany silently roll,
"they made the oxygen in your lungs, the roof over your head,
the bed you sleep on, the table where you eat, the paper you wipe…"
She says, "I know. I know. You're like the Lorax.
You speak for the trees,"
and then, "Remember, how I used to make you
read it to me every night for like a year?"

After Timber Junction sweeping curves
that echo Wolf Creek's forested bends.
Steeply up again to the highest summit
then down and down over Quartz Creek

through the active slide, the road always being rebuilt,
past the Elderberry Inn over the Nehalem again
glimpse the logging relics at Camp 18
then up once more.

Mile Post 14 to 11
From Douglas Summit we descend into cloud-bank,
Sitka spruce comes in.
My chain-smoking professor of botany said,
"Where the fog goes, *sitchensis* grows,"
draws water through needles not only roots—
roots, dug, gathered, twisted,
woven by the Haida and Tlingit
into tight baskets, waterproof hats.
I'd like one of those
to replace my favorite cap,
lost last winter to the wind at Cape Falcon
flicked off and whirled away,
spun down and down to the surf raging the rocks
at the foot of Cape Falcon.
Farewell.

In St. Petersburg, Russia, Gustav Heinrich von Bongard studied specimens
collected by a Karl Heinrich Mertens, botanist
on the Russian ship *Senyavin* on its survey of Alaska, 1829.
Karl died suddenly, at 34, after a voyage to Iceland;
what killed him so young: sepsis, appendicitis, pneumonia?
This was fifty years after Cook sailed to Sitka
with spruce bud beer, a ration against scurvy;
on his return to the Big Island,
some Hawaiians took a liking to a small boat,
to ransom its return Cook tried to take their king hostage,
instead was clubbed and stabbed,
killed in the surf with two marines.
The Hawaiians knew he was no god, just a petulant sailor —
three lives for a boat   no cooling peace of trees that day.

Mile Post 11 to 6
I crack the window: sun-warmed needles,
marine air, melting tar and hope my wife's right,
"Just a stage…she'll see the forest and the trees again."
Von Bongard lumped the tree with pines,
but later, in Paris, that self-taught farm boy,
Éli-Abel Carrière, sorted out the conifers,
knew it was *épicéa*, spruce.

Picea started here, northwest North America,
then branched east, west:
Engelmann, Norway, White,
Black, Green Dragon, Colorado Blue.
Single needles, tiny knives,
its boughs defend against curses and spells.
The wood is light and strong,
Orville and Wilbur built their planes with spruce.
Tight-grained old growth esteemed
for tone wood in mandolins, fiddles, guitars,
the soundboard at the heart of a piano.
Makes good pulp for paper, its cellulose
collapsing into long sturdy strands.
Wood like moonlight through fog,
the deep gray bark, the platy flanks
of long extinct fish swimming skyward,
soft-scaled, sand-colored cones
easily looted by Douglas squirrels.
When my daughter was younger
she and the neighbor kids gathered
the stripped cores, "squirrel tails" and
traded them for the hard pitchy branch roots
dug from the red "meat" of rotting logs,
used as swords or guns or horses for dolls.

Many of those dead and down
were lying in these woods when I was a kid;
takes a century or two for a log
to be wholly dismembered and remerged
with the living.

Mile Post 6 to 3
The road levels onto the coastal plain,
we near the grave of the giant Sitka at Klootchy Creek,
biggest in the U.S. while it still stood.
I'd like to stop, look, touch its bark again,
but my daughter would only whine.
The top was sheared off in the gale of 2007,
a few years later the county dropped the remaining trunk
to protect us frail humans from falling spruce chunks.
It had no low branches to lay down, set root, and sprout anew
like "Old Tjikko" in Sweden, a 10,000-year-old Norway spruce.
I'd like to visit that re-re-re-resurrected *Picea abies,*
Scandinavia's Christmas tree.
Hope she will come with me this December,
as every year before, to cut one for our Christmas
—not picea, needles too prickly, a fir instead.

She falls back into herself,
like rain filling a creek bed at the end of a dry spell,
"Battery's dead but we're almost home,"
she says and watches out the window.
Tomorrow I'll spend all day in the woods:
bushwhack down into that draw I saw the other day
to check that stand of spruce for the new record holder,
click teases at the squirrels,
Wonder at how spruce roots grow so tangled.
I couldn't even trace one from tip to tree
without getting exquisitely lost.

I'll look up their steep trunks
to the ceiling of needles for a glimpse of blue,
over the up-curled bark scales, so dry, so long out of water.

Mile Post 3 to Home
My lumbar is starting to clench after two hours driving,
"Did you know," she asks, "that Reagan didn't really say
"If you've seen one redwood you've seen them all"?
What he really said was, "A tree is a tree. How many more do you
    have to look at?"
"Same idea," I tell her.
"No, he was trying to balance trees with people. If you protect
    every tree
then loggers like my friends' dads are put out of work. How do they
    feed their families?"
I tell her, "He also said that trees cause more pollution than cars."
"Really?" she asks, gets quiet, then says,
"I feel sorry for what happened to him, well, more for his family
…how he was lost to Alzheimer's."
I ask her, "Are you becoming a latter-day Reaganite?"
"No Dad, just a human."

I swing the car through the last turns then accelerate up the
    final hill;
our house comes into view, then the dark spruce beyond,
I can't wait to get out of the car,
head out into them, walk the tightness out,
breathe in the moist tang of sea and pitch,
I say aloud, "Sitka spruce, where you grow, I go."
She glances over with a puzzled look then sits up,
smiles.

A Boy Found a Body

Klootchy Creek Wayside, near Seaside, Oregon

Raven, flying downstream in the mist before dawn,
passes over the hole in the canopy that the old Sitka rose above and
    filled;
the branch she used to land on near the top and throw her call out
    into
      the fog
lies under the leggy sprawl of elderberry.

Coho salmon returning up the Necanicum
would ascend the riffle, ease around the bend and into the pool
where Klootchy Creek comes in.
Some would rest, others would dig their redds in the gravel
and spawn: eggs the color of red huckleberries spilling out
into that dappled shade.
Its roots easily reached this far
taking in water and decaying bodies of spent salmon.

I arrive over the one-lane bridge just off the highway,
from the parking lot you can see the only vertical remains
a 30' stump shedding the last of its bark,
pock marked by woodpeckers.
A granite slab says the name is Cloutrie not Klootchy,
Antoine, early Seaside entrepreneur,
was leading some timber cruisers up the river in April 1899.
They went missing.
While out rambling the woods a boy found a body—one of the
    cruisers,
searchers found the rest,
last of all Antoine clutching a can of beans on a log,
"ptomaine" poisoning clenched their guts and killed them all.

There is another plaque with timelines and photos of the tree when
    it still stood,
500 to 750 years, heart-rot erased some rings: oldest tree, oldest
    living thing, in Oregon.
Was.

First the lightning strike—a spiraled gash
that opened the trunk to the weather,
then the windstorm that split it wider.
Rotten chunks came falling out.
The following year hurricane winds broke it there.
Elderberry thrives in the opening,
covering the old Sitka's shattered body.
People still stop here, look, and drive on.

Tell the Story Back

Chapter by chapter, ring by ring
to the sapling's center O
the sprout tip pressing up through moss
rain softening the seed,

David,
when you woke to rain on the roof
the morning of your last day
did you recall
your first bawling breath
how before that
you floated
in the warm thrum
of your mother's amnion sea?

Washing the Corpse

On washing the corpse, we found it in a shocking state: there were
ten to twelve gashes on the head, a long one over the left eye, another,
rather deep, just above the left temple, and a deep one behind
the right ear ; the left cheek-bone appeared to be broken, and also
the ribs on the left side. The abdomen was also much bruised,
and also the lower parts of the legs.

—FROM *ACCOUNT OF DOUGLAS' DEATH IN THE SANDWICH ISLANDS*

Ashes

Fraxinus

… we put up on the south side of a muddy stream, banks covered with
Fraxinus. No deer killed this day, although several were seen.

—DAVID DOUGLAS

Ash Street, Alderbrook, Astoria, Oregon

My dog is sniffing
marking every clump of grass
as we walk the River Path
along Astoria's rivered edge
causeways weedy with grasses
and horsetail, stork's bill, cat's paw
blackberry, ivy, vetch
two cormorants fish in fog below the trestle
an eagle perches on a weathered piling
an entire tree hammered deep into the riverbed.
On the mudflats a great blue heron stands poised to spear a meal.

Thinking, how some names are deeply rooted
others have crowded in like weeds
I don't know the ancient Clatsop name for this place
perhaps no one knows it anymore
instead it's *Astoria*, for John Jacob Astor
who never saw it, lost a fair bit of his fortune
trying to wedge into the fur trade here.
Why not name it *Coboway,* a Clatsop chief,
or *Celiast,* his daughter, who
after marriages to a French fur trader and a missionary
lived her last years here
living the Indian Way
speaking only the Clatsop tongue

We follow the path into Alderbrook
where there is no brook but plenty of alders
it would have been better named Alderslough or Alderbank
three streets wide along the river an ABC of trees
there are seven cedars on Cedar Street
on Birch Street is one weeping birch
white bark poxed by mildew
but there are no ashes on Ash Street
yet another name not tethered to its place

The Genus Ash

Ashes, kin to olives, lilacs
without the fruits, the plumes of flowers
trees of balanced symmetry, branches always opposite
a cormorant, wings outspread to dry
the odd numbered leaflets of the compound leaves
feathers of some enormous verdant bird
come even when split down the center shaft

Straight trunked in youth
the heron vigilant at water's edge
before the gnarl and lean of age

Winter-bleak, with all its plumage molted
so stark and seeming dead what prayer would bring
a fallen god's rehabitation, reverse this doom
rinse its roots, recharge the phloem
return it full-feathered to the height of green?

Limbs that rise and dip like wings
but never soar in breeze or gale
each seed sealed in its thin samara
when loosed will sail equal to any wind

Ash Wood

Before the missile   the bullet
before the bullet   the arrow
before the arrow   the spear
ash wood best
one end sharpened then hardened in fire
later fitted with a deadly head of bronze then stronger iron
thrown or thrust in bloody hand-to-hand
neck pierced
thigh run-through
Gore or be gored

Ash still used in modern battles:
cricket stumps and bails,
in baseball
bottom of the ninth
three runs down, two outs, bases loaded, full count
the fast ball strikes the sweet spot
on the swung bat's barrel
rebounds flies
out of the park

Ash wood prized too for less heroic tasks
flexibility married to strength
handles for hand tools
axe adze shovel hoe hammer
younger wood best
older trees
favored for shapely canopies
summer shade

The ashes of North America and Europe
the green, the white, the blue, and black
the *Oregon,* the common *excelsior*
will fall like the chestnut, like the elm

as the emerald ash borer spreads its range
its larvae chewing tunnels through the inner bark
scribbling out the cambium leaving each tree
to desiccate

An Ash I Know

May go the way of that ash of whom
the Elder Edda's sooth-sayer, seer, the Vala, spoke

A great ash I know grows in a northern dale
stands always green so lovely in morning dew
Ashtr Yggdrasil, Ash Tree Odin's Gallows
where Odin hung wounded by a spear
sacrifice of himself to himself
to gain deeper powers

Odin's spear formed from the wood of Yggdrasil
never missed its mark
Yggdrasil   with limbs so wide
A horse could walk along them
its roots drawing from Mimir's well
from the Hel of those who died dishonored
branches widening into homelands
of elves, dwarves, giants
their traits braided in with ours
the thick trunk reaching to Asgard
realm of the old gods
doomed at Ragnarok the end-time when

All will be at war
brothers shall slay brothers
sisters' children shall stain their kinship red

Yggdrasil quivered shook leaves thrown loose
scattered far
its great trunk groaned
fire raged a forest of flame blanking out the stars
and the World sinks in Ocean

In time
Earth rises, dripping, green and new
high up an eagle glides in search of fish
Yggdrasil did not fall or fully burn
two humans hid within a hollow in its trunk
Lif and Lifthrarsir
Life and *Life's Body*
and so the last become the first

Kindling

That new world
is now old
and you
having severed yourself
from yourself
felled all that is whole and holy
the great tree leans it cracks keens
feel the trunk strike earth
Thor hammering hammering
hammering his enemy
before he dies himself

you halve its trunk
and halve each half
and halve each half of half
then tip the rounds flat to split
cleanly cleave each one
swing the axe again again
again so much kindling
to feed your fire

What comes after its embers?
sink now
cease

ashes
   ashes
      we all
         fall

Buds

drifts of pink-white petals
on the forest floor
needle duff
leaf-mold
shed tinder

cast away

blossoms of bitter cherry
leaves of vine maple
spruce tips

the message sent
through sap
Open, flare, unfurl
your duties now begin

warmth after winter's cold
the gift of water
the folded form within

Road Floods During Rain

Sunt lachrymae rerum et mentem mortalia tangunt
—Virgil, *The Aeneid, Book I*

David,
Easy to find Kawaiha'o Church in Honolulu
built of slabs of coral hewn from ocean reefs
and its shady graveyard
where you are buried in an unmarked plot.
Only a bit harder to find, inside
in the dim corner beneath the stairs to the balcony,
your weathered marble plaque all but illegible,
a bronze tablet below it now
reprising the Latin inscription, its translation
of your birth in Scotland, your indefatigable travels,
your sacrifice to science in the wilds of Hawaii
on your third visit there,
ending with that quote from Virgil:
   E'en here the tear of pity springs
     And hearts are touched by human things
I prefer Heaney's translation
   There are tears
     at the heart of things
Lost both parents that year, yes
there is grief enough for all.
The church was empty, except for us, cool
despite the midday sun,
the ebb and surge of traffic
dampened by its coral walls.

But David,
I didn't make it to your death site on the Big Island:
Ka lua kauka, Doctor's Pit,

a short hike off Mana Road,
where there's a monument and a grove of Douglas-fir.
The pit is gone—why Doctor's Pit I'd wondered,
then found you were adept at mending wounds, setting fractures,
like Menzies before you.
Guides I read said:
four-wheel drive recommended (but not required) for Mana Road
So I reserved a Toyota 4Runner for a day
when I went to pick it up
the guy at the desk told me,
"You're on your own for Mana Road…."

"What's it like?" I asked.
He said, "Never been on it."
We laughed.
Thinking, well, hoping, it would be a rough one-laner
with a few steep and rutted spots,
I decided to go ahead, I already owed the rental fee.
Mana Road was that and more
10 mph in 2nd low
contouring the flank of the dormant volcano Mauna Kea
the 17.7 miles to the trailhead
would take a couple hours. Then the hike, the drive back…
An intermittent mist became a light but steady rain.

David,
you would have recognized the gorse
from your childhood in Scotland,
invasive here, hedging out the grasses,
arrived and spread after your visits.
At Mile 6 the first sign:
"Road Floods During Rain"
ruts and chunks of lava to dodge
trickles, rivulets, small streams channeling the dirt,
dips and ruts filling up.

David,
It rained like this, soft incessant shush,
when my sister and I
walked the grounds at Scone Palace the next year in May,
where you were gardener,
train from Edinburgh across the Firth of Forth,
along the coast then inland
to Perth on the River Tay,
you know the way,
"Longest in Scotland,
carries more water than the Thames,"
our cabbie proudly told us.

Highland cattle, sleeping in the rain,
albino peacocks, foraged under oaks,
we skipped the Palace tour and took a wide path
past the chapel where the kings and queens of Scotland
were once crowned,
through an arch in a rock wall to the Pinetum
planted with conifers you sent back
western hemlock and red cedar,
sequoia and redwood, a Douglas-fir
lower branch wide as a torso
held out like an arm
bark smoothed where many
have bellied up and sat.

A forest of giants
outsiders at home in cool, wet Scotland
like us, both our parents' fathers' families
emigrated from towns east of here
passed through them when I was seventeen.
My memory a few unwritten postcards:
the church in Friockheim

where my mother's father's father
was baptized.
In Cupar my father's distant cousin,
a pharmacist, red-cheeked,
smiling over tea.

David, there is a new gazebo
just beyond the kitchen garden
with maps of your travels,
the portrait that seems to be
in every book about you
and a hand-carved Douglas-fir cone
hanging from the arched rafters like a chandelier
the size of Billy, your loyal Scottie.
Did one your native guides
tell you the tale of how your tree
saved the mice from a great fire?
After all the other trees had turned them down
Douglas-fir let them dive into the shelter of its cones
The seed bracts are their hind legs and tails
sticking out from their hiding places.

Perhaps you heard a second part when
after the flames' scorch and singe had passed
the mice turned tails for tongues
to taste the air for rain,
and when it came they took the seeds
they shared their shelters with and
forgoing their hunger,
carried them out into the burn,
tunneled through the rain splattered ash,
and planted them.

At Mile 10 another sign
bottom of a steep grade

a deep puddle covering the entire road.
Beyond, the road rising again
a snake of water steadily delivering more.
Not wanting to get stranded or
end up with a thousand-dollar tow bill,
and with my daughter, in the back seat, complaining
about how long it would take to get there and back
for just a short stupid hike.
and how she had a headache gearing down on her
from all the bouncing…
I decided to err on the side of caution and peace
and turned around.
bouncing back to the paved road,
to the year of doctor's appointments
the surgery.

David,
When I return to Hawaii Island
I'll hope for no rain, a smoother road,
better luck   than yours.

Each Name

each name a path into the grove
that hides and holds the spring
where roots en-web, find tongues
to drink, to talk of
woods
after clear cuts and 2,4-D
forests
before the first stone axe
gashed bark
bit sapwood
I know I know
the name is not the named
so wide the water between those shores
so how can I ever hope
to unearth each root tip
see forest and tree

Still I seek each name
not taxidermed, filed in dark herbariums
but breathed with in the canopy first dawn of summer

each a whittled ode
that carves us to its shade
the truth of water
osmosing into roots lifted to lighted leaf
reborn as vapor, rain

how in chlorophyll's crucible each
whirls magnesium draws in nitrogen
enraptures sun

how each assembles cambium
bundles xylem, phloem
flows the sweetened sap
and speaks

touch wood
trust
be anchored
bend to the wind

Acknowledgements

I would like to thank the journals that first published early versions of the following poems:

A Boy Found a Body; Red Alder; West Through the Coast Range
North Coast Squid

Ashes; Bark; Cones; Planted Pines at Second Point
Green Linden

Elegy for Western Redcedar; Radicle
Rain

Cedars: True or False
In Layman's Terms

Log Yard
Windfall

Naming the Tree
Written River

Roots
Turtle Island Quarterly

Tree, Its Roots
Fib Review

Quotations from *"Hávamál"* and *"Völuspá"* of *The Poetic Edda* are adapted from translations by Olive Bray, Ursula Dronke, and Benjamin Thorpe.

Quotation from *Gilgamesh* is adapted from translations and versions by Andrew George, Stephen Mitchell, and N.K. Sanders.

David Douglas' quotes and the excerpt from "Account of Douglas' Death in the Sandwich Islands" are from *Journal Kept by David Douglas During His Travels in North America 1823–1827* (1914).

For more on David Douglas' life I highly recommend Jack Nisbet's *The Collector.*

A huge thank you to Bob Pyle for his encouragement and generous help in getting this book published.

About the Photographer — Nathan Wirth

Using a variety of techniques—including long exposure, infrared, intentional camera movement and the occasional dip into compositing—Nathan Wirth seeks to express his unending wonder for the fundamental fact of existence. In his work, he attempts to photograph the silence he believes can still be experienced in our ever-increasing world of auditory and visual noise. Nathan, who was born and raised in San Francisco, earned both his Bachelor of Arts and Master of Arts in English Literature from San Francisco State University and brings a deep appreciation of poetry to his explorations of place (especially the sea).

COLOPHON

Touch Wood is typeset in Dante with titling in Albertsthal
Typewriter and Whitney. Since the rise of the industrial mania,
the world has lost around three trillion trees, cutting their global
proliferation almost in half. The editors of Watershed Press
are proud to publish James Dott's elegiac yet compassionate
extension to our arboreal kin of Confucius's demand
that "first we rectify the names." First printed in
the late summer of 2025 in an edition of 100 copies.